GARFIELD
IN THE ROUGH

BY: JIM DAVIS

BALLANTINE BOOKS · NEW YORK

ISBN: 0-345-32242-8

Designed and created by Jim Davis
Illustrated by Gary Barker
Manufactured in the United States of America

First Edition: October 1984

1 2 3 4 5 6 7 8 9 10

CAMPING SUPPLY GUIDE

50 lb. bag of kitty litter — no fuss, no muss — sanitized and completely biodegradable.

Fully stocked refrigerator — camping is always more fun when you take your best friend.

Garlic clove talisman — to insure the campers "King of the Hill" superiority in the food chain cycle.

Microwave oven — plus 200 miles of extension cord.

Credit cards — for the motel in case the weather is anything but perfect.

Telephone — camper can constantly stay in touch with his agent, lawyer, accountant, broker, pizzeria, and suicide prevention hotline.

Inflatable easy chair.

AM/FM cassette forest blaster — to assist the New Wave camper in break dancing across the forest floor.

Campers own bed... to insure that no roots, rocks, sticks, or stems interfere with a good weekend's sleep.

Headphone set — to tune out those distracting sounds of nature.

Gas grill — for barbecuing small woodland creatures that forage too close to the camp site.

Pocket coffee maker — this compact morning eye-opener is also wash 'n wear.

Pocket blender — for blending roots, herbs, and berries with your favorite ice cream.

Electric can opener — a must for the campers who can't hunt, fish, or trap.

Color TV — for tuning in old Tarzan movies to enhance the camping experience.

REST AND RELAXATION!

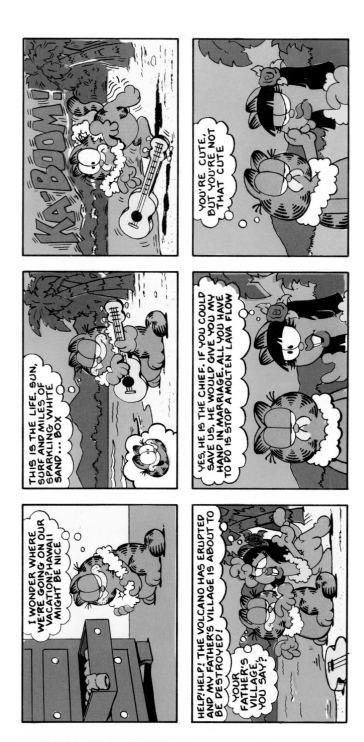

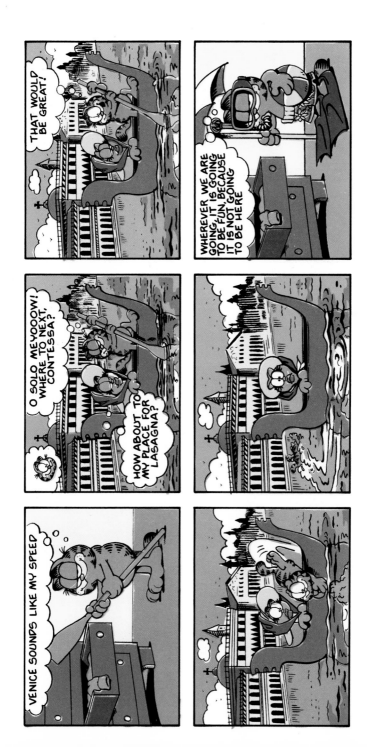

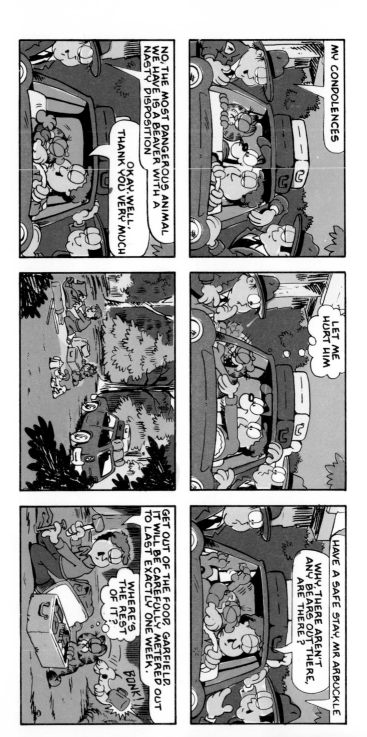

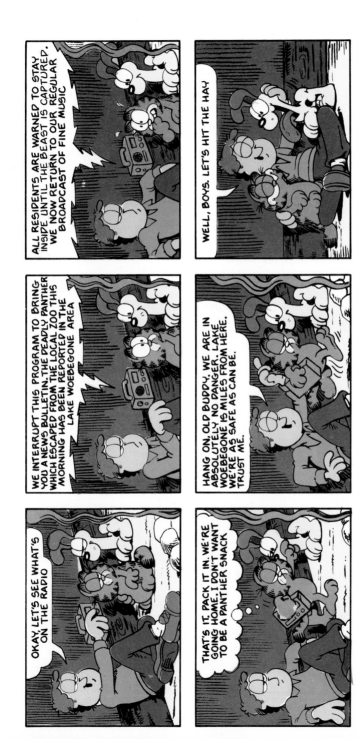

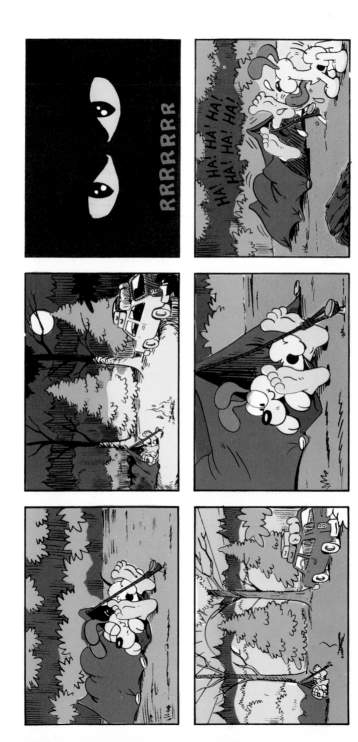

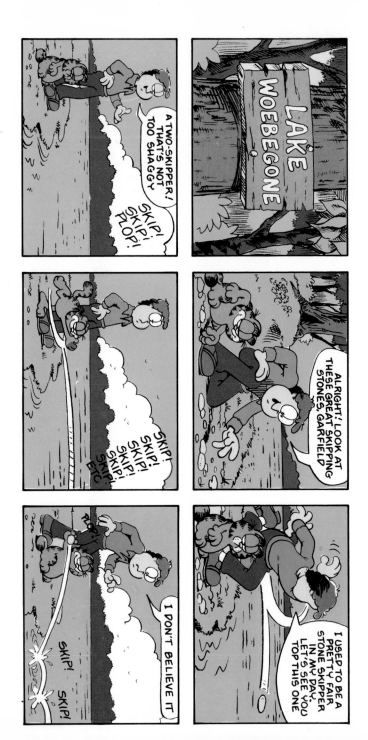

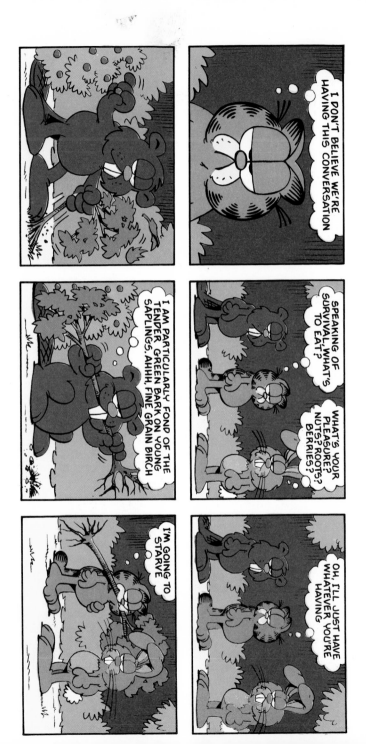

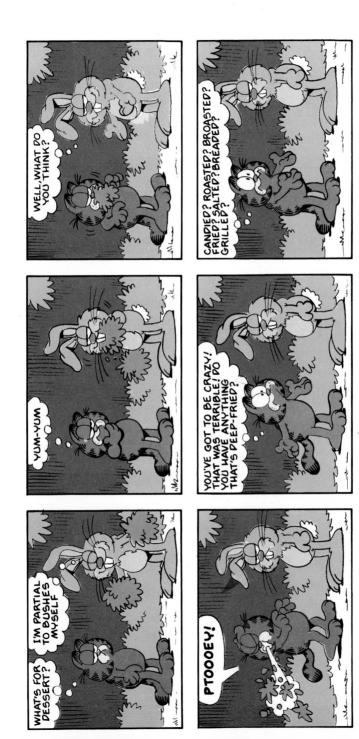

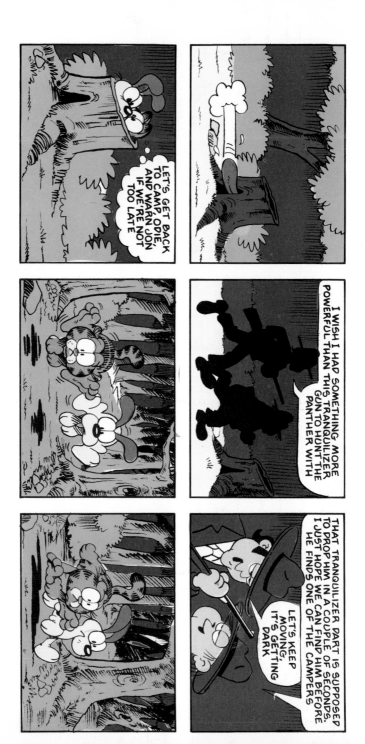

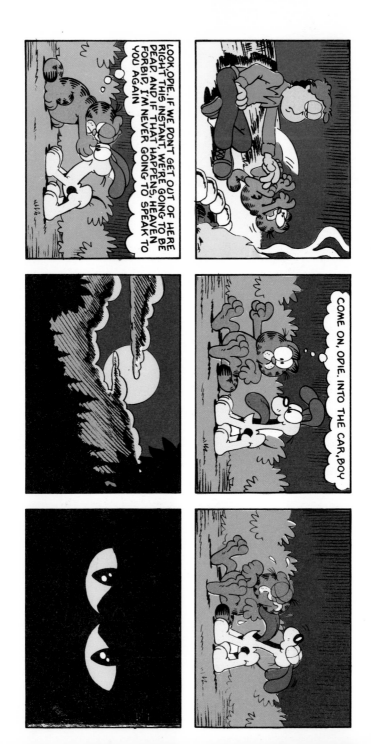

RRRRRR

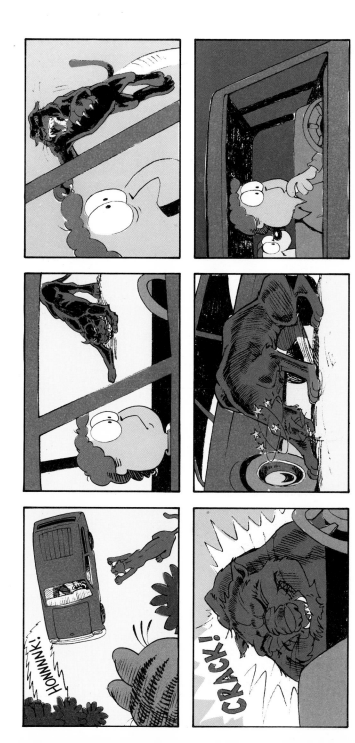

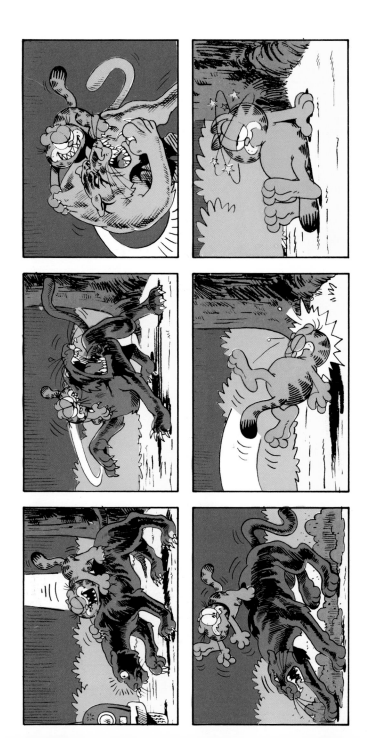

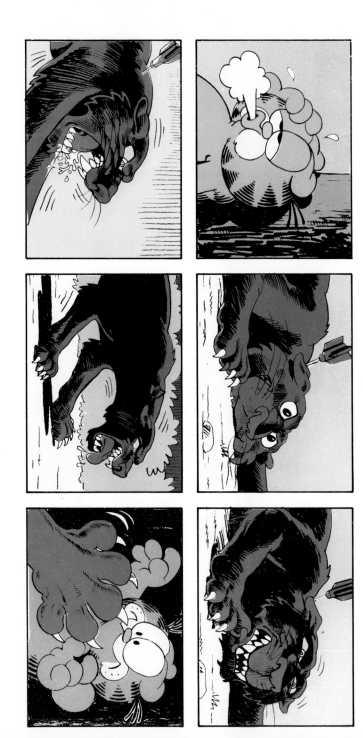

Steps in Making an

1. *Story:* The writer selects a theme (Christmas, camping, etc.) and develops the story. The characters are introduced and taken through the plot in a series of gags and situations. (Everything is resolved in the end.) A finished script is then supplied to the producer.

2. *Storyboard:* A storyboard artist draws the story in a form similar to a comic strip and establishes story continuity, action, long shots, closeups, etc.

3. *Recording of Voices and Songs:* After selecting the proper voices for the characters and the songs to be used, they are recorded on ½ inch magnetic tape.

3A: *Reading the dialogue and music:* The tracks are transferred from ½ inch tape to 35 mm magnetic film. A film editor "reads" the track frame by frame to indicate the position of each letter and word or music beat.

4: *Directing:* The director times the picture out scene by scene to the required length. Using the track readings supplied by the film editor, he makes out exposure sheets in preparing the scenes for the animators. The required action and dialogue is indicated on the sheets frame by frame.

5. *Layout:* The layout artist designs the picture. He or she establishes the style of design to be used. Using the storyboard as a guide, the layout artist composes each scene regarding the characters' relationship to the background, props, etc.

Animated Film

6. *Animation:* Using layout poses and the exposure sheets with the director's instructions, animators bring the characters to life. By sketching the characters in a sequence of several drawings, the animator can create many moods and attitudes.

7. *Background:* The background artist renders the layout sketches in full color and sets the color styling.

8. *Checking:* The checker coordinates the animation, layout, and background areas and prepares all animated scenes for ink and paint and for camera.

9. *Ink and Paint:* The animators pencil drawings are transferred on to celluloid sheets (cels) by either Xerox or hand tracing by inkers. These cels are then painted on the reverse side by painters. Putting the drawing on cels allows the background to show through when the cel is superimposed over it.

10. *Camera:* Using the exposure sneet as a guide the cameraman shoots the drawings in each scene on film one frame at a time as indicated by the animator.

11. *Editing:* The film editor assembles the picture as indicated by the director and adds sound effects and background music.

12. *Dubbing* (Mixing): Up to this time there are separate dialogue, music, and effects tracks. Here they are combined into just one track. The dialogue, music, and effects are set at their proper level throughout the picture.

13. *Answer Print:* The film lab issues a final print with fully balanced color and soundtrack.